I0480850

Lead by Faith

"As you grow as a Leader, Your Business Grows"

Shiketa Morgan

Forward by LaShonda Plair

Shiketa Morgan Publishing and Coaching

First Printing, 2021

ISBN 9798713509989

Printed in the United States of America

Dedication

This book is dedicated to all the business owners that continued to lead by faith as we moved through the 2020 pandemic. We made it through by Faith.

Contents

Foreword

"You must lay out your plans in faith and be willing to accept where they take you."

Faith is an anchor, and it must be rooted at the start of your journey. Most definitely a journey of leadership.

You must have a faith plan in place prior to execution, prior to communicating it and prior to stepping into a path. Furthermore, it's an unseen project that only you can see through the eyes of God.

Once you trust the process, show ability to lead with standards, GOD will open the doors of Growth. I can attest to this process because this was me 17 years ago in my career.

I didn't understand why God lead me to QSR. I had people tell me that it's just a chicken job. But GOD had a bigger plan for me. I had to humble myself, I had to pray for understanding, believe in the mission and trust the process.

 I walked away from a 9 to 5 with weekends off and with no understanding of why. I accepted a 50-hour week salaried position in a hectic region, with a team of limited leadership experience with no vision or plan to win.

I often went home wondering what I did. I must admit I didn't pray a lot then, however I had deep-rooted foundation of faith.

I went back to my roots which was the business of daily communication with God. This elevated my team and I to the next level.

After thinking my growth was halted, God stepped in an answered my prayers. I watched a failing area become profitable and people with no vision level up and become leaders.

For 17 years I have passionately led by trusting God knowing that the result would be a win! This happened by prayer, faith, and a daily commitment in the process of leading.

Trust the process of faith, it will lead you to the top.

LaShonda Plair
Regional Franchise Director East Region, QSR

Introduction

"A Journey through Leadership"

The year was 2003 and my Children and I were at a Photo day at our local church. I saw my pastor at the event, and he said to me, *" Hey sis how is business?"* I replied, *"You didn't tell me how hard it is to be a leader."* My pastor at that time was (Bishop Larry J Baylor of Faith Miracle Temple in St. Louis Missouri) he said, Y*es, I know leadership is hard"* and he asked me if I ever heard of John Maxwell and I said no.

Bishop Baylor invited me to attend the Leadership classes at church and due to my busy days at my childcare facility, I could not make the classes. However, I decided to take Bishop Baylor's advice and I bought every John Maxwell book that I could read on leadership.

As I began to read John Maxwell books on leadership, I realized this: *"If you want to be a great leader, you must develop your character."*

When I opened my first childcare center in 2003, I was so surprised to see how challenging it was to lead other people.

In fact, I struggled with getting the staff to do what I needed them to do and to be quite honest, I began to resent moving the business out of my home.

My staff turnover was horrific. I hired all the wrong people and hiring the right staff was one of my biggest challenges in business.

However, I know today that my hiring challenges that I faced in 2003 were a result of my lack of leadership skills and an indicator that I needed some leadership training.

In my home daycare, I was used to working alone and I did not have the people or leadership skills that I needed to influence others and to motivate others.

Furthermore, as I pressed on by faith, with lots of counsel and studying leadership; my turnover was reduced, I began to love having employees. Most of all, I was a happier leader and I absolutely fell in love with reading leadership books.

 In this book, I will share stories from my leadership journey along with wisdom that will inspire you to keep leading by faith as you grow as a leader.

 Also, I hope that as you read this book, that you have many aha moments and after reading this book, that your faith as a leader *grows.*

Shiketa Morgan

ARE LEADERS BORN OR MADE?

According to Psychology Today, the most asked question about leadership is: *Are leaders born or made?* In fact, the author of the article, Ronald E. Riggio, PhD said that research indicates that "Leadership is about one-third born and two-thirds made."

As I reflect on that research, it caused me to think back to my childhood. Being the oldest child has tremendously contributed to my characteristic as a leader. As the old oldest child, I was expected to set an example for my younger sibling. Furthermore, being expected to be the example for my siblings, caused me to develop a belief that I must set a high standard for myself and others as a leader.

 In fact, my mother was extremely strict with me and she did not allow me to hang out much with my friends and she seem to always talk to me often about my choices and making decisions that would impact the rest of my life.

I can honestly say that the standard that was set for me along with my upbringing contributed to how I lead my team and how I carry myself as a Leader.

I may have been a born leader; however, two-third of my leadership abilities was still not developed when I became an employer.

In fact, I was able to see that I needed to develop my leadership skills, when I expanded my Business in 2003.

Furthermore, I believe that one of the best things that I could have done on my leadership Journey was develop the leader within me, because even a born leader… ***needs developing!***

Before I bring this chapter to a close. I want to share more insight with you that has been inspired by the following question: ***Are leaders born or made?***

According to the Jack Welch management Institute, "The answer to the born leaders' question isn't neat or simple. The facts are, some leadership traits are in-born, and they're big whoppers. They matter a lot. On the other hand, two key leadership traits can be developed with training and experience—in fact, they need to be."

Jack Welch also believes that there are essential traits that a leader has, and they are as follows:

- Positive energy: the capacity to go-go-go with healthy vigor and an upbeat attitude through good times and bad.
- The ability to energize others, releasing their positive energy, to take any hill.

- Edge: the ability to make tough calls, to say yes or no, not maybe.
- The talent to execute very simply, get things done.
- Passion. They care deeply. They sweat; they believe.

As I read through those leadership traits recommended by the Jack Welch Institute, I believe that those are the main ingredients to true leadership.

Furthermore, I believe that those are characteristics that can even be developed through lots of coaching and developing.

Let me ask you a question: Did you see yourself in any of the leadership characteristics above? If so, I want to challenge you to take some time to reflect on your natural leadership abilities that you were born with and take some time to journal about the essential traits that Jack Welch believes that a great leader has.

If you find that you have some leadership traits that need to be developed, don't worry. I believe that as you read this book, you will activate many of the leadership traits that lay within you.

All you must do is start working on the traits and you will be on your way to becoming a Dynamic Leader!

BUILDING YOUR FAITH AS YOU LEAD

Leading others has been one of the hardest things that I have ever done. In fact, I can remember when I opened my first childcare center in 2003.

 I struggled with the thought of quitting every day for about 10 years. However, it didn't take me long to realize that Leadership is truly a Faith walk, because my Faith gave me the courage to keep going.

Furthermore, I discovered that when you make the decision to not quit and keep moving forward, no matter what it looks like, that you will become a Leader of Big Faith.

In this chapter I am going to share with you several stories that tested my faith and inspired me to keep leading by faith.

In 2005, I heard a knock on the door of my 1st childcare facility. I opened the door, and it was a tall man with an Internal Revenue badge. When I opened the door, I said: *"How can I help you?"* He replied, I'm looking for Shiketa Morgan.

 I'm sure I turned very red in the face, because that was so embarrassing to have an IRS agent to show up at the business mid-day and we were fully staffed.

I thought, oh my God, He must be coming to collect the $5,000 in taxes that I owe. So, I invited the IRS agent to step into my office.

Once we were settled in my office, the IRS Agent began to explain to me that several notices had been sent to the business and He asked me how would I like to pay the bill?

I did not have the money, however, I asked if I could make a payment arrangement. To make a long story short, I was forced to sacrifice over $1200 a month until the debt was paid.

That was clearly a defining moment on my business Journey and on that day, I realized it is not wise to ignore a notice that you receive from the IRS. Today I make monthly tax deposits on time and a payroll company generates all my quarterly tax returns.

That IRS agent visit was an embarrassing moment; however, it was a necessary part of my leadership journey. In fact, it helped me to stand during tough times, make tough decisions and move on by Faith.

In January 2018, I retired as a Child Care Center Director and I hired a woman that had over 20 years of experience in the childcare industry. When I hired her, she seemed like a strong leader and I knew she was the best person for the position.

I spent over six months working side by side with her and at one point I felt like I was in her way so I backed up and allowed her to show me what she can do as a leader. She was great at building enrollment and coordinating events and was a great trainer.

In the summer of 2018, my husband and I decided to step out on Faith and move to Atlanta. We had previously visited Atlanta in 2013 and moving to Atlanta had been a desire for over five years.

Furthermore, I thought with the right leader in place and the business was very established, we could relocate to a new city. Several months after we moved, all was well.

My husband and I began to look for a location in Atlanta, along with managing our St. Louis location from Atlanta, we were traveling back and forth from Atlanta to St. Louis to check on our Business.

Then about four months into the move- *something shifted.* Several of my long-time employees began to resign. In fact, I had an employee to tell me, you inspired me to live my dream and I am going to pursue a new career.

I began to wonder if I made the right move. So, I took all the changes in the business to God in prayer and I prayed for divine direction.

One of the things that God showed me was that things never stay the same and the people that start out with you, may not finish the Journey with you.

As I began to let go of how things were seeming to fall apart, the plan was really coming together for my good. In fact, that move to Atlanta taught me to let Go of trying to control the outcome and trust God.

In 2019, my second location was not making much money and we struggled with finding the right staff. I decided to close that location and merge both locations.

Closing my second location was one of the best business decisions that I could have ever made. In fact, the day that we closed that location was one of the happiest days of my life.

The inspiration to close that location came to me one day as I sat in my prayer room. As I sat in my Prayer room in April 2019, I was looking at one of my plants and I noticed that the plant was full and vibrant looking. However, there was one dead leaf on the plant.

As I cut the leaf off the plant, I heard in my spirit to cut anything away from my business that could kill the whole tree.

That was the day that I decided to close my second location. My second location brought me the most stress, it had the highest staff turn-over and it was just not where I wanted the business to be.

So, I made the decision to cut it off the tree, save money and merge the schools. That decision gave me so much peace and I have no regrets. As you can see, Leading by Faith involves making lots of tough decisions and not worrying about what anyone thinks, but God.

A Leader that walks by Faith, has hope, confidence, and courage. Most of all, trusting and believing that all is well, no matter what it looks like.

I want to share with you six ways to build your Faith as a leader:

1. Lift your Business Endeavors up to God in Prayer. After all, it is God that gave you the gift of Business.
2. Make the decision to not quit no matter what it looks like.
3. Let go of wanting to control the outcome. You can only control you and what you contribute to the process.
4. Read inspirational books that build your Faith.
5. Dream Big for your Business, commit your dream in prayer to God and don't give up on the dream!
6. No matter what it looks like, keep your cool and know that it will all work together for your good. Every situation has a purpose. Trust the process and Keep leading by Faith.

"A Leader that walks by Faith, has hope, confidence and courage."

GROWING AS A LEADER

CONSISTENT GROWTH IS KEY TO GREAT LEADERSHIP.

~ JOHN MAXWELL

Working as a Child Care Center Owner and Director was stressful the first five years and it was because I was still growing as a leader. As I struggled as a Leader, it had a major effect on the business. As I mentioned in the previous chapter, my staff turnover was extremely high, I had little trust in my staff, and I tried to do everything myself.

In fact, I was not used to letting others help me to carry out the vision in my heart and having that mindset only caused me to struggle as a leader. When I realized that my leadership skills were affecting the business, I began to read Leadership books and get advice from my mentor.

My mentor during the first five years of owning a center was a lady by the name of Mary Krogmeier. She was a wonderful mentor. One of the things that I loved about Mary was the fact that she asked me a lot of questions. Her questions caused me to think and it helped me to think outside the box. When I would tell Mary about my business challenges, she would simply say, Shiketa, you need to choose your battles!

That statement taught me that every business battle is not worth fighting.

As I worked on myself as a leader and began to grow, my staff turnover improved, people loved working for me, and I began to enjoy being an employer. In fact, I found that your attitude is your biggest attribute as a leader and the people that follow you will catch your attitude.

I used to wonder why I kept attracting employees with negative attitudes and then I realized it was because I had a poor self-image and my attitude needed lots of work. I can remember buying a book by John Maxwell titled: Attitude 101. That book changed me on a business and a personal level. In fact, I have also used that book as a training tool for my lead teachers. And I saw a tremendous change in my team as we read that book together.

A Positive Attitude is Everything!

Furthermore, I have found that the more that I grew as a leader, I was also inspired and empowered to develop those individuals that are in my circle of influence. Also, as I grew as a leader, I was inspired to keep growing my business and growing the people that I lead, because a business can only go as far as your ability to lead.

" Everything rises and falls on leadership."

Five Ways to Grow as a Leader

1. Read leadership books by successful people that have a proven track record in leadership.

2. Attend an annual leadership conference to gain fresh leadership insight.

3. Journal about your leadership Journey. This is a great way to reflect and look within yourself. You will more than likely find the solutions to your day -to - day problems as a leader, *simply by Journaling.*

4. Get a mentor. Someone that has been where you are seeking to go. No need to learn from experience when you can learn from someone else's mistakes.

5. Develop your people skills. *Business is 80% people skills and 20% Business knowledge.*

Please allow me to share a brief story with you.

I used to have a bad habit of wanting to change things around in mt childcare center. In fact, I used to change the classrooms every week. One day, a parent came in the building and said: *"why do you all change the classrooms around so much?"* I was offended that she asked that questions, because at that time, I thought, *it's my business and I do what I want to do!*

However, the question that the parent asked, caused me to take a closer look at why I wanted things to change the classrooms all the time. After much reflection, I realized that this was a bad habit of mine that I brought into the business and I didn't realize how my habits had a major effect on the business.

Early childhood research also shows that too many changes can affect the behavior of the children. Once I discovered that too many changes affected the children, we now only change the classrooms once a year.

Something else that I learned from making too many changes is this: " *It is difficult to trust a leader that is constantly changing things."*

That situation with the parent, also taught me that you can grow by simply paying attention to what others say about your business and your leadership.

Also, try not to be easily offended by the opinions of others, simply use the question or comment as an opportunity to *Grow!*

As a leader I find great pleasure in sharing books that have added great value to my Leadership Journey, and I am going to share seven of those books with you:

1. Develop the Leader Within You by John Maxwell

2. Winning with People by John Maxwell

3. The Positive Dog by Jon Gordon

4. Martin Luther King Jr on Leadership by Donald Phillips

 5. The Power of Positive Thinking by Norman Vince

6. 4th Dimensional Living in a 3- Dimensional world by Dr. David Cho Young

7. The Law of Confession by Dr. Bill Winston.

I also want to challenge you to read a new leadership book every month to increase your capacity as a leader.

Moreover, I want you to know this: ***Your business will only grow to your capacity to lead.***

So, if you plan to keep growing your business, I want to encourage you to keep reading.

A Nation that Reads much, Knows Much.

~ Thomas Jefferson

BECOMING A FOCUSED LEADER

" Success isn't magic or Hocus Pocus, its simply learning how to Focus." ~ Jack Canfield

Leadership has taught me so much about the power of Focus. In fact, I have learned that whatever we focus on grows. This includes the good and the bad.

As a Child Care Center Director, I would always tell the staff to Focus on the behavior that they wanted to see repeated in their classrooms. For example, if you see a child running, praise the child that was sitting and following directions. Then watch how quickly the child that is running, stops running because you gave the child that was doing the right thing your attention. A child seeks attention just like our problems do, but remember, only what you give your attention will grow.

Moreover, focus is just that simple. Focus on what you want to grow, *and it will grow*. Also, whatever you stop focusing on will not grow.

In the book, The Power of Focus, Jack Canfield listed 10 Focus strategies with the first strategy being:

Your Habits determine your future. (The quotes that you see in the next three pages are excerpts from Jack Canfield's book) *" If you keep on doing what you've always done, you'll keep on getting what you always got."* Jack Canfield also wrote:

"Successful people have successful habits, Unsuccessful people don't!"

As you can see, your ability to focus will impact your effectiveness as a leader. Moreover, I have discovered that the more that I have on my plate, the more focus that I need.

In fact, as my business grew, what I focused on every day determined whether I had a productive day, or not. My goal is to help you to have more productive days after you read this chapter, because your role as a Leader will be so much more fulfilling when you intentionally choose what you focus on each day.

" Once a new habit is well developed, it becomes your new normal behavior."

Are you ready to develop some new focus habits and new behavior that leads to a great level of focus as a leader?

If so, Let's dive right into 10 habits to becoming a focused leader:

1. Plan your day before it starts. If you start a day without a plan, you have already planned to have an unproductive day. Tip: Get a planner and plan your business week before it starts.

2. Focus on your top priorities the first part of your day.

3. Schedule a time to read email and to post on social media. ** Don't let social media steal your precious time.

4. Delegate the duties that give you a lower payoff and do more of what bring you the greatest reward.

5. Study the lives of successful and focused people, because success leaves clues.

6. Turn off your cell phone if it is a distraction and return calls when you have some free time. Tip: Only take calls if it is an emergency. If you were on a job, your boss wouldn't let you answer the phone all day, because your boss wants you focused on the work at hand.

7. Keep your vision board some place where you can see it. Your vision should be your motivator to stay focused on your business goals.

8. Check in with your planner mid-day to see if you are on track with accomplishing your daily priorities.

9. Return important phone calls before you end your business day.

10. Listen to a motivational podcast or audio to help you to stay inspired as you work.

So, what do you think about the habits that I just shared with you in this chapter? Are you inspired to take-action? Are you inspired to do something different so that you get different results?

I know the habits above may seem like a lot, however, once the habits that I shared with you become a habit, you will do all the above without even thinking about it.

It's time to get focused.

Stay Focused and Keep Leading by Faith!

EQUIPPING THE LEADERS AROUND YOU

"A LEADER'S SUCCESS CAN BE DEFINED AS THE MAXIMUM UTILIZATION OF THE ABILITIES OF THOSE UNDER HIM." ~ JOHN MAXWELL

Over 10 years ago, I bought a leadership book written by Leadership Guru John Maxwell titled: **Developing the Leaders around you**. In the first chapter of the book, John Maxwell wrote about the importance of raising up potential leaders.

In fact, in that first chapter, John Maxwell wrote: "*The Key to surrounding yourself with other leaders is to find the best people you can, then develop them into the best leaders they can be. Great leaders produce other leaders.*"

Are you ready to develop the leaders around you? If so, I want you to know this: *when you take the time to develop the leaders around you, you are simply equipping your team to help you go to the next level!*

In 2005, I was starting to feel overwhelmed and exhausted as a leader. Furthermore, I couldn't understand why it took so much energy to manage employees and it seemed like my team depended on me for everything.

Then I heard about John Maxwell's book, *Developing the Leaders around you*. That book inspired me to start developing the Lead teachers in my childcare center and when I took the time to develop the leaders around me, my job as a Center Owner and Director was not as stressful.

Also, I discovered that when I had leaders around me; I was more effective as a business Leader. Moreover, I realized that the key to growing a business was having leaders that could run the business without me always being there.

Furthermore, I realized that I was frustrated as a leader for many years because I was hiring followers and when I would hire a great leader, I did not know how to nurture the leaders.

In the book, Developing the Leaders around you, John Maxwell, listed 10 qualities to look for when hiring a leader and they are as follows:

1. Positive Attitude.

2. The willingness to serve.

3. The potential the grow

 4. The determination to do their job.

5. Loyalty

6. The ability to bounce back when trouble arise.

7. Trustworthy

8. The ability to see the big picture.

9. The ability to work whether you are there or not.

10.Thankful heart

As I listed at the qualities above, I must say that I agree that every good leader has all the above qualities.

In fact, the big question is this: *How do you see all of this at the interview process?* The answer is: you will not see all these qualities during the interview process; However, I know who has seen those traits; **_A previous employer!_**

Therefore, it is important to call the previous employer and check the track record of potential leaders, because, if the previous employer can confirm that your potential applicant possesses all 10 of the traits that I listed on the previous page; I can honestly say that you have a great candidate for a leader in your company.

Once you begin to select leaders for your business, it is vital that you develop a plan to nurture your leaders.

When I began to nurture and equip my leaders, it was as if I had reproduced myself. In addition to that, it is a great feeling to train the leaders around you, so that you can go to another level in your business.

People are more motivated and productive when they are nurtured and trained to do a great job.

Here are seven ways to equip and nurture the leaders around you:

1. Build trust by being consistent. Also, never speak negative about your staff.

2. Be transparent...admit your mistakes and work to correct your errors.

3. Spend time with your leaders. Go to lunch or dinner on a regular basis and connect with them.

4. Believe in them. When you believe in people, they strive to make you proud.

5. Encourage the leaders around you.

6. Set growth goals and mentor your leaders. Sending your leaders to an annual leadership conference is a great way to invest in them.

7. Share your Dream. Your dream is what motivates why you do what you do; and people want to know where they are going and why they do what they do.

" Having the right players determines 60-80% of the success of any organization." -Bob Biehl

I believe that after reading this chapter that you are ready to equip, nurture and motivate the leaders around you.

In fact, if you are in a season of growth, it is vital that you take the time to develop the leaders around you, because as your team grows...*Your Business will Grow!*

" Men are developed the same way that gold is mined. Several tons of dirt must be moved to get an ounce of gold. But you don't go into the mine looking for dirt. You go in looking for gold."

~ Dale Carnegie

LEADING LIKE A PILOT

*" A Pilot has excellent leadership skills and is very
detailed and knows how to focus under pressure."*

Before the Covid19 pandemic, I frequently travelled
to the airport once a month from Atlanta to St. Louis
for Business.

While I was at the airport, I noticed the following de-
tails:

1. Airport employees seemed extremely focused
   on serving the travelers.
2. The boarding process was incredibly detailed.

In fact, As I would wait to board the plane, I would
watch for the pilot to enter the plane. I loved to see the
pilot get on the plane, because this was my point of
reassurance. Furthermore, if the pilot didn't look like
he or she did not appear to have a sound mind, *I was
not going to board that plane!*

I believe the Pilot's role is the most important role on
the airplane because the success of the flight is solely
depended on the leadership skills of the pilot with the
help of a co-pilot.

In fact, to be successful as a Pilot, you must be detailed orientated and able to focus under pressure.

Also, according to a job description listed on (Better-team.com) a pilot's responsibilities includes:

- Performing pre- and post-flight inspections of fuel, equipment, and navigational systems.
- Operating the aircraft safely and maintaining a good degree of professionalism
- Monitoring weather conditions and communicating with air trac control.
- Determine the safest routes and analyzing flight plans.
- Anticipating issues
- And keep up to date on aircraft advancements and equipment.
- Updating and reassuring passengers and flight attendants in the event of an emergency.
- Liaising with co-pilots and flight crew throughout the flight.

As you can see, a Pilot plays a vital role in not just flying the plane but reassuring everyone that is on the plane.

I am almost certain that it takes a dynamic leader to be able to Fly an aircraft, stay focused, keep everyone on board reassured when there is turbulence in the air and always maintain a professional attitude.

I was inspired to write this chapter after sharing "My Leading like a pilot principle" with my leadership team.

In the meeting, I simply described myself as the air control tower, because I send instruction from Atlanta to the Pilot in St. Louis (who is my center Director) and the Co-pilot (my daughter who is the secretary).

My leadership team really liked the analogy, and it gave them a clear understanding of their roles as the pilot and the co-pilot of the plane (which is the child-care center).

After we talked about the role of the pilot and the flight attendants, there was lots of discussion about training and the importance of having skilled child-care workers on board (who were our flight attendants, and the children are the passengers).

Then, I ended the meeting with this question: *"What do you think will happen to the plane if the Pilot and the Co-pilot stops listening for instructions from the control tower (me)?"*

There was a long pause and then some laughter. Then they said, *OMG! the plane will crash!!* That was Exactly what I was thinking and at that moment, I felt like there was a greater understanding of the power of having focused and detailed oriented leadership on board.

Tips for Leading Like a Pilot

- Pilots always look great.
- Flight attendants always look great and are very professional.
- The Pilot's voice has a way of soothing the passengers.
- Always make your Passengers (Your customers feel special)
- Serve your passengers well.
- Train your Flight attendants well (your employees)
- Stay focused and give regular updates to your passengers and flight attendants.
- Get enough rest.
- Handle all emergencies with calm.
- Before the flight, greet the passengers so that they can see who oversees the plane.
- Stay in communication with the air control tower and the co-pilot.
- If there are clear skies communicate it. If there is turbulence communicate it. Never stop communicating!
- Be a lifelong learner, develop your confidence and stay focused!
- If you give someone else the role of being the pilot, be sure that you play the role of the control tower and send orders that will keep the Business from crashing.

MAKE YOUR HEALTH A PRIORITY

"BELOVED, I WISH ABOVE ALL THINGS THAT YOU PROSPER AND BE IN HEALTH, EVEN AS YOUR SOUL PROSPERETH." ~3JOHN 1:2

My health has not always been a top priority. In fact, my Church, Family, and my Business were my top priorities for many years. Moreover, eating healthy and self-care days were not on my priority list twenty-two years ago when I started my business.

However, I didn't place a priority on my health until I began to feel the effects of stress from running a Child Care Center. Owning a Child Care Center can be very demanding.

In fact, my days as a Center Director were full of dealing with staff issues, making decisions for the business, handling parent concerns, operating in multiple roles and many days running errands along with lots of paperwork.

The first time that I realized that I must relax and have some selfcare days was when I noticed I began to forget especially important things. In fact, I was even forgetting names of customers.

That forgetfulness concerned me, and I began to do some research on stress and the mind.

What I discovered was that multi-tasking was bad on the brain and chronic stress causes memory issues. So, I decided to have a self-care day once a week by scheduling a Swedish massage every week and I became fascinated with the power of essential oils.

 Relaxation became a lifestyle for me, and I became a more relaxed and calmer businesswoman. The relaxation did not slow me down at all. In fact, my weekends were very relaxing, however my weekdays were very busy.

During the week, I did the grocery shopping for the center, I helped to drive the vans and so much more.

In 2007, I was carrying a watermelon into the center, I bent over and felt a sharp pain in my lower back. Several days later, I could not sit.

So, I went to the Emergency room. My blood pressure was elevated, and the doctor wanted to do an X-ray of my back. The X-ray exposed that I had a ruptured disc in my lower back and the doctor ordered some physical therapy.

That back pain impacted me for about 6 months and came along with taking pain medication. I was then forced to work part time at the center, because sitting was almost impossible along with getting in and out of the car.

During that time, I began to reflect on my stress levels and my duties at the facility. Once my back healed, I became fascinated with reading health books. One of my Favorite health book authors is, Dr. Don Colbert. Dr. Don Colbert is a **certified medical doctor focusing on Family Practice and anti-aging medicine in Florida and Dallas**, **Texas**. Dr. Don Colbert is also a New York Times Best Selling Author and has written over 40 health and wellness books, over the past 30 years.

As I began to read and study Dr. Colbert's health books, I began to eat more fruits and vegetables. I developed a heart healthy diet, and I ate less foods that contributed to pain and inflammation in my body. Most of all, Dr. Colbert inspired me to drink more water.

As a business Owner, it is vital that you eat healthy and develop a relaxation plan, because it makes no sense to build a business that you cannot physically enjoy.

I became fascinated with health because I saw firsthand how your health can affect your quality of life and business Journey. Moreover, I have learned that if you don't make your health a priority, you will be forced to with an unexpected health issue.

My love for health and wellness led to me hosting healthy family events at my childcare center and in my home, because I literally believe that your health is your wealth.

In 2016, my dream of operating multiple locations became a reality. I gained 6 new employees, a second childcare center that was already operating and I found myself being terribly busy again.

Within a year of managing two childcare facilities, my weight increased because I began to slack on eating the foods that I knew to eat. In between visiting my sites, I would stop and buy fast food.

One day I was sitting at my desk and I felt my heart skip a beat. I notified my doctor's office immediately and the nurse instructed me to come in for a blood pressure check.

During my doctor's office visit, I discovered that my blood pressure was elevated, and my doctor started me on a low dose blood pressure medicine. I was not happy to take blood pressure medicine, however, I knew I had to take it easy, so I went part time again in the business so that I could focus on my health.

On New Year's Eve in 2017, the back pain returned. I thought, maybe it was my high heel shoes.

My friend suggested that I go see a chiropractor and I did. The chiropractor ordered x-rays and the X-ray results were devastating to hear.

The Chiropractor called me into his office, and he said to me, *"You have arthritis in your lower back."*

I thought, you have got to be kidding me! Then I thought, I'm only 43 and I have arthritis. I shared my diagnosis with a few family members, and I found out that many of my family members also had arthritis, but that did not inspire me to not do anything about the arthritis diagnosis.

Shortly after being diagnosed with arthritis in my back, I began going to the Chiropractor three days a week. The pain was so bad, and I thought it would cripple me, because I had an extremely hard time going from a sitting to a standing position.

However, with prayer, more diet changes, chiropractor care, I am pain free today and I take no more arthritis medication. That season of my business Journey taught me that you not only have to build your business by faith, but you must take back your health by faith.

Furthermore, I realized that the stress was starting to manifest in my body; and it was time to focus on creating a schedule that allowed me more time with my family and more time to relax.

Once My center directors showed me that they did not need me full time at the centers, I also, took some time to eliminate the wrong foods from my diet and I had to get my emotions under control.

Operating two centers, was not the problem, I had a problem with letting go and managing my emotions when it came to handling issues in the business.

As my back healed and I worked on healing my emotions, I delegated more duties to my center directors, I was able to return to operating the centers without any pain and today I am still working part time from home.

As I bring this chapter to a close, I want to share with you some things that I did to help me to lose the unwanted weight, manage my stress levels, lower my blood pressure, and helped me to get rid of the inflammation that was causing the arthritis and they are as follows:

1. Stay hydrated by drinking lots of spring water.

2. Go for a 30–45-minute walk daily.

3. Relax more.

4. Take some time daily to meditate and don't let the emotions of others become yours.

5. Eat lots of fruits and vegetables.

6. Avoid fried foods. They are bad for the heart and they cause inflammation in the body.

6. Get an annual physical and know what is going on with your body.

7. Know your family history and don't assume because a disease runs through your family blood line, that you should claim it. Do whatever you can to overcome sickness and disease with lifestyle changes.

8. Avoid eating junk foods like chips and candy bars every day. When you eat junk food, you feel like what you eat. ** Its ok to enjoy life and have some sweets periodically.

 9. Eat healthy snacks daily like air popped popcorn, hummus, avocado dip, carrot sticks, apple slices, almonds, walnuts, etc.

If you want to be a healthy business owner, it is vital that you let go of wanting to control every detail in your business, make the decision to eat healthy and think healthy thoughts.

I hope this chapter has inspired you to make your health a priority as you build your business and Lead by Faith.

If you have experienced any health issues, my prayer is that you take your health back by Faith!

" Your Health is your Wealth."

LEADING THROUGH TOUGH TIMES

THE FORCES THAT THREATEN TO NEGATE LIFE MUST BE CHALLENGED BY COURAGE....THIS REQUIRES THE EXCERCISE OF A CREATIVE WILL THAT ENABLES US TO HEW OUT A STONE OF HOPE FROM A MOUNTAIN OF DESPAIR.

~ DR. MARTIN LUTHER KING

Leading through tough times will build your faith if you simply find the courage to keep leading. In fact, leading through tough times is when you will simply discover how much Faith that you have as a Leader.

Furthermore, tough times have a way of stretching you as a leader and causing you to dig deep inside for that courage that you didn't know that you had.

As I write this book, we are in a pandemic. This Covid-19 pandemic has forced many businesses to operate at a 50% or lesser capacity and many businesses closed due to the pandemic.

Moreover, this pandemic has forced many businesses to operate at a level of creativity that we have never seen before, however, if you want to survive during a pandemic; it is vital that you get creative and keep moving forward by Faith.

During the 2020 Pandemic, many business owners, just couldn't find the courage to keep moving forward in a pandemic and they took the pandemic as a time to retire or close their businesses.

I decided to take a different approach. The 2020 pandemic only pushed me to develop a ***bounce back mindset!***

I took some time to look back at all the other seasons that God brought me through, and I found the courage to keep the doors of my childcare center open during the pandemic.

Even though the childcare industry was hit hard by the Pandemic, I did not allow the pandemic to cause me to make fearful business decisions.

I moved forward my Faith and with the mindset that families need our service and if parents needed us, the doors were open with strict health guidelines.

During the pandemic, two of my employees contracted COVID-19 and it forced us to briefly shut down twice during the pandemic. Closing the center to clean and allow families to quarantine; cost us over $18,000. However, I had to make a decision that would keep the children and staff safe.

I trusted God and I was able to gain access to an SBA Disaster loan and a government payroll protection plan that helped to provide extra working capital for the business as we kept the center open during the pandemic in 2020.

I have seen many challenging days as a business owner and as I mentioned at the beginning of this chapter, it is the tough times that develop your faith.

One of the greatest leaders that I know lead the world through very tough times and his name is Dr. Martin Luther King Jr.

In 2019, I visited the Dr. King center in Atlanta, Georgia and I purchased a Book from the Ebenezer Baptist church titled: *Martin Luther King, Jr. on Leadership.* Chapter 15 of the book is titled: ***Having the courage to lead.***

In chapter 15, the author (Donald T. Phillips) wrote about principles that Dr. King used to lead us through a tough time, and they included:

- Turning the other cheek
- Having Faith
- Keeping your sense of humor
- Turning a negative into a positive

As you can see, even Dr. King believed that it takes Faith and many other strategies to lead through tough times. In fact, that entire book was loaded with leadership Inspiration and wisdom for tough times, and I want to share some of that wisdom with you:

1. Your job as a leader is too great, and the days are too bright to be bickering in the darkness of jealousy, deadening competition, and internal ego struggles.

2. There is nothing to be afraid of if you believe and know that the cause for which you stand for is right.

3. Courage breeds self-affirmation. It faces fear and thereby masters it.

4. Remember that the road ahead will not always be smooth.

5. There is no painless way to have a revolution.

6. A refusal to be stopped, the courage to be, the determination to go on despite, the hallmark of great movements.

7. Seek to transform your suffering into a creative force.

" Somebody is saying stand, so I guess I'll have to stand."

~Dr. Martin Luther King

LEADERSHIP WISDOM KEYS

*WISDOM IS THE PRINCIPAL THING, GET IT
AND IN ALL YOUR GETTING, GET
UNDERSTANDING." ~ PROVERBS 4:7*

According to Proverbs 3:19, God needed wisdom to lay the foundations of the earth and God needed wisdom to establish the Heavens. Then Proverbs 3:20 indicated that by knowledge, the depths were broken up and the clouds drop down the dew. ***How powerful is that!***

In fact, I believe that if God needed wisdom to establish this beautiful earth, we will also need wisdom and knowledge to build a successful busines by Faith. Most of all, to Lead by Faith.

King Solomon was one of the riches and wisest men to ever live and according to King Solomon, wisdom is gained from God. In 1King, God came to Solomon in a dream asking Solomon what He wanted, and Solomon asked God for.... ***Wisdom***. Not only did God give Solomon wisdom, but God gave Solomon riches, wealth, and honor.

Can you relate to Solomon's request? I'm sure there probably has come a time on your Journey as a leader, that you needed lots of wisdom.

In fact, I know that I have. I have asked God for wisdom before hiring employees, before I signed a new lease and I pray for wisdom daily, *because Wisdom is the principal thing.*

There are several other ways to get wisdom for your business Journey and they are as follows:

- Trying new things
- Talking to other experienced leaders
- Make mistakes (experience makes you wiser), and read books written by successful leaders.

As I mentioned before, I pray for wisdom daily, however, I gained lots of wisdom from the books that I read.

I have hundreds of books in my home library, and I can honestly say that reading books has provided me with lots of wisdom for my business Journey.

Over the years, I have read many leadership books that has inspired me. I went through my home library and I picked 10 books that inspired my leadership Journey.

I pulled 10 Wisdom Keys from the books and I will share them with you today:

Wisdom Key #1

If you want to build a great enterprise, you must have the courage to dream great dreams. ~ Howard Shultz/ Pour Your Heart into it

Wisdom Key #2

Being positive really is a Choice and feeding the positive dog inside you is one of the most important choices you can make. ~ Jon Gordon/ The Positive Dog

Wisdom Key #3

Let people know that you need them because people need to be needed. ~ John Maxwell/ 25 ways to win with people.

Wisdom Key #4

Let your team know why you placed them on your team and what contributions you expect each member to make. ~ Mary Shapiro/ HBR Guide to Leading Teams

Wisdom Key #5

Once you identify potential leaders, you need to begin the work of building them into the leaders they can become. ~ John Maxwell/ Developing the Leaders around you

Wisdom Key #6

Be more concerned with your character than your reputation because your character is what you really are, while your reputation is merely what others think you are. ~Pat Williams/ Coach Wooden

Wisdom Key #7

Life is growth, I said. "Business is Growth. You grow or die." ~ Phil Knight/Shoe Dog (A memoir by the creator of Nike)

Wisdom Key #8

As a leader, the energy you put into your team and culture determines the quality of it. Research from the heart math institute shows that when you have a feeling in your heart, it goes to every cell in the body, then outward-and people up to 10 feet away can sense the feelings transmitted by your heart. ~ Jon Gordon/The power of positive Leadership

Wisdom Key #9

Self-awareness and self-love matters. Who we are is how we Lead. - Brene Brown/ Dare to Lead

Wisdom Key #10

Dreamers are often misunderstood. Dreamers provide jobs and income for those who refuse to dream. They stretch the imagination of everyone around them. They thrust average people into the zone of greatness. ~ Mike Murdock/Secrets of the Richest man who ever lived.

Be obsessed with obtaining wisdom.

LEADERSHIP PRAYERS & AFFIRMATIONS

" PRAYER INVITES THE POWER AND THE PRESENCE OF GOD IN YOUR BUSINESS."

I start every business day with prayer. In fact, every Sunday I commit my entire business week to the Lord in prayer.

My personal prayer time has helped me to tap into the divine side of doing business and I can honestly say that God has given me wisdom from above through my prayer life.

The bible also tells us that if we decree a thing that it shall be established unto us and that Life and Death is in the power of the tongue. Therefore, I believe that confessing positive words over your business daily is so powerful.

In this chapter, I have included prayers that you can pray before expanding a business, hiring new employees, making decisions in your business along with making declarations over my business.

" Rejoice always, pray without ceasing, give thanks in all circumstances, for this is the will of God in Christ Jesus for you." ~ 1Thessalonians 5:16-18

Prayers for Business Growth

Father God,

I thank you for giving me the grace to grow my business. I thank you in advance for prospering my business. Most of all, I thank you for sending an anointing that will lead to Good Success and Business growth. Now lord I ask that you strengthen my hands to build my Business and give me the mental capacity to handle Business growth.

In Jesus name,

Amen

A Prayer for Leadership

Father God,

I thank you for entrusting me to lead your people and I ask that you lead the way. Most of all, I ask that you give me the grace that I need to be a supportive and encouraging leader to the people that you have assigned to me. Furthermore, help me to lead my employees and my team that gives you glory and honor.

In Jesus Name,

Amen

A Prayer for Tough Times

Father God, I thank you that you have brought me this far and I ask that you give me the grace that I need for this season of my Leadership Journey. Also, I ask that you fill my mind with the knowledge of your will and give me divine peace that will help me to endure this season.

In Jesus Name,

Amen

Leadership Declarations

Decree a thing, and it shall be established unto you…

Declarations #1

I am a confident and

courageous Leader.

Declaration #2

I am growing bolder and confident every day.

Declaration #3

God leads me and as God leads me, I follow

Declaration #4

I attract great employees to my business.

Declaration #5

I walk by Faith and not in Fear or Doubt.

Declaration #6

I am a positive and excited Leader.

Declaration #7

I grow in Wisdom, Favor and Stature daily

Declaration #8

I lead with a spirit of excel-
lence.

Declaration #9

I am slow to anger and Fast to Pray.

Declaration #10

I expect to have daily divine encounters and divine connections daily.

CONCLUSION

As I bring this book to a Close, my prayer is that you are inspired and empowered to Lead by Faith. In fact, my prayer is that this book has added great value to you as a Leader. In fact, my goals for this book were simply to inspire you to build your Faith as a Leader, inspire you to be a focused leader, inspire you to Lead like a pilot, focus on your health, give you strategies for leading through tough times, provide you with the wisdom that you need to Lead and inspire you to become a Leader of Prayer.

So, let me ask you several questions. How has this book helped you? Are you inspired to keep leading by Faith? What have you gained from this book? What do you plan to do differently after reading this book?

Please take a moment and write down your answers and start implementing the take always that you gained from this book. I believe that when you start implementing what you have learned from this book, that you will activate your Faith as a Leader and you will begin to see the changes that you desire to see. Until we meet again, keep walking by Faith, Trust God on the Journey and the best is yet to come for you.

Shiketa Morgan

ABOUT THE AUTHOR

Shiketa Morgan Owns a Child Care Center, she is an Inspired Author and Business Coach. She lives in Atlanta, Georgia and is from St. Louis Missouri. She is married, a mom and has some amazing grandchildren. Shiketa has self- published over 17 books and is the founder of the Child Care Business Owner Institute blog where she inspires and empowers Child Care Business Owners to build successful childcare businesses. Shiketa has big faith in God and knows first - hand that when you put God first in your business, you are destined to *Grow and Succeed!*

BOOKS BY THIS AUTHOR

Build Your Business by Faith

Principles for building a business by Faith, including: Thinking Bigger, Letting go as you grow, how tithing brings increase and so much more.

The Inspired Business Woman

This book will empower you to go from stuck to inspired. Principles in this book includes facing your fears, strategies for doing more of what inspires you, tips for developing your focus and so much more.

7 Keys to Managing Multiple Locations

This is a book about what it is like managing multiple childcare locations and strategies for developing systems, along with business growth strategies.

Child Care Business Expansion Guide

This book provides you with strategies to successful expand a Child Care Business. Great book for a home provider or a center owner.

10 Steps to Starting a Child Care Business

This book is a step-by-step guide to starting a home-based childcare business or a center.

The Art of Owning a Center

The guide to Owning a Child Care Center. Tips that will empower you to build a Successful Child Care Center!

For more Child Care Business eBooks, click here:

e-Books | The Child Care Business Owner Institute

Shiketa's Doing Business by Faith Coaching Services

Sign-up for a Doing business by Faith Empowerment coaching session today. In the session, you will be inspired to build your Faith for Business success.

In a 1- hour Doing Business by Faith Empowerment Session with Shiketa, you will discover:

- How to Find the Courage to Dream Big
- How to Speak Faith Filled Words over your Business
- How to Fill your mind with Faith Thoughts
- How to overcome the temptation to Quit and how to defeat self-sabotaging thoughts
- How to Use Prayer and the word of God to Build a Prosperous Business!

Are you ready to Activate your Faith and start moving in the Direction of your Goals and Dream for your Business?

If so, sign-up below, because it is time to Activate your Faith for Business Success!

www.shiketamorgan.com

Child Care Business Coaching

I have owned a Family Home Child Care Business and two Child Care Centers. I know what comes with owning a Child Care Business and it is vital to your Business Success that you have the Support of a Business Consultant or Coach. *That's why I created Individualized Child Care Business Coaching Options!*
In my Coaching Sessions, I share my Business secrets and strategies with you, and I Commit to coaching you through any Business challenges that you may be facing!

Coaching options include:
- How to start a Child Care Business
- How to expand a Child Care Business
- 1-hour Business Strategy coaching session.

Sign-up today at: Coaching | The Child Care Business Owner Institute

Doing Business by Faith Podcast

Be sure to subscribe to Shiketa's Doing Business by Faith podcast and be Inspired to build your business by Faith.

Doing Business by Faith • A podcast on Anchor

Contact Shiketa Today

To book Shiketa for an in-person or a virtual Speaking engagement, please contact Shiketa today by sending an email to:

shiketamo@gmail.com.

Connect with Shiketa on Social Media

Facebook

Shiketa Morgan Coaching (facebook.com)

Instagram

www.instagram.com/shiketamorgancoaching

Twitter

www.twitter.com/shiketamorgan

www.twitter.com/ccarebusiness

Blogs

www.childcarebusinessowner.com

www.doingbusinessbyfaith.com

Website

www.shiketamorgan.com

Keep Leading by Faith!

www.ingramcontent.com/pod-product-compliance
Lightning Source LLC
Chambersburg PA
CBHW070504220526
45467CB00002B/575